USA TODAY. **TEEN WISE GUIDES**
A GANNETT COMPANY

LIFESTYLE CHOICES

HEALTH
SMARTS

How to Eat Right, Stay Fit,
Make Positive Choices, and More

MATT DOEDEN

TWENTY-FIRST CENTURY BOOKS / MINNEAPOLIS

Note: Neither the author nor the editor of this book are physicians. None of the content in this book should be considered medical advice. Always check with your doctor before making changes to your diet or exercise regimen.

Twenty-First Century Books
A division of Lerner Publishing Group, Inc.
241 First Avenue North
Minneapolis, MN 55401 U.S.A.

Website address: www.lernerbooks.com

Library of Congress Cataloging-in-Publication Data

Doeden, Matt.
       Health smarts : How to eat right, stay fit, make positive choices, and more / by Matt Doeden.
              p.   cm. — (USA TODAY teen wise guides: lifestyle choices)
       Includes bibliographical references and index.
       ISBN 978-0-7613-7023-9 (lib. bdg. : alk. paper)
       1. Teenagers—Health and hygiene. I. Title.
RA777.D64 2013
613'.0433—dc23   2011041280

CONTENTS

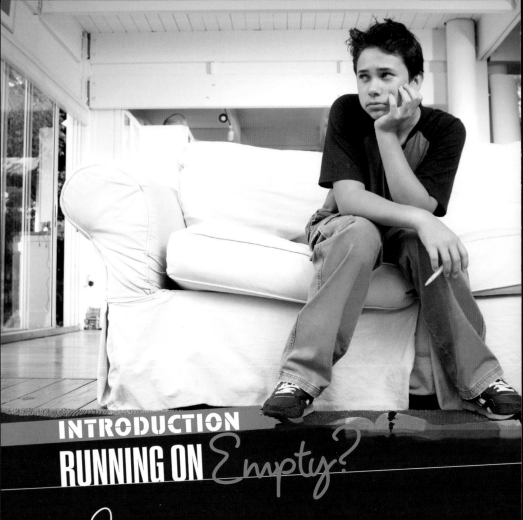

RUNNING ON *Empty?*

*I*t's past midnight, and you're still cramming for your big history test. You're munching on potato chips and slurping a soda, doing everything you can to fight off sleep. You've been locked in your room since after dinner, and you've got a long way to go.

But your mind is wandering. You find yourself reading the same page over and over again, but none of the information sticks. You're worried about soccer tryouts next week. You're wondering what you should buy your best friend for his birthday. You're distracted and exhausted.

Cheese puffs and soda may give you a quick burst of energy, but choosing nutritious foods will help you feel nourished for the long-term.

Does any of this sound familiar? Your mind and body are capable of remarkable things. But to get the best out of them, you've got to treat them right. Eating nutritious foods, exercising regularly, and getting plenty of sleep are just the start to living a healthful and productive life. If you find yourself in the situation like the one described here, you may not be leading a lifestyle that will help you be healthy, productive, and successful. But there's good news: even a few simple changes can make a world of difference! Keep reading and learn more about the kind of lifestyle that will have you set to succeed!

1 HUMAN BODY 101

Your body needs regular exercise and good food to function properly.

What's the most complex piece of machinery you own? It's not your laptop, your plasma TV, or your smartphone. *It's your own body!* Your body is also the most important machine you own. Think of your body the way you'd think of a finely tuned sports car. It's capable of amazing things, but only if you treat it right. Like a sports car, your body needs quality fuel (food) to run. Also like a sports car, your body needs regular maintenance. For example, you have to exercise your lungs, your heart, and your muscles if you want them to function well. And you need to see a doctor for checkups or when you're sick, just like you'd take a car to a mechanic.

Sports cars, smartphones, computers, and other machines usually come with instruction manuals. But you've got no such luck when it comes to your body. You've got to learn for yourself how to care for it. And there's one critical way that your body isn't at all like a sports car: if your car breaks down, you can always replace it. You don't have that luxury when it comes to your body. You're stuck with the one that you've got—so it's important to take care of it!

BUILDING A BODY

It may sound strange, but you've built your own body, almost from scratch! When you were conceived, your entire body was made up of two microscopic cells—one from your mother and one from your father. Those two cells combined and immediately started to multiply. Two cells became four, four became eight, and so on. Within about twelve weeks, your body was already about 2 inches (3 centimeters) long and contained all your major organs! By the time you were born, your body was probably somewhere around 20 inches (51 cm) long and weighed in the neighborhood of 7.5 pounds (3.4 kilograms). That was quite a growth spurt, and it was only the beginning!

Your cells multiply and you continue to grow from the time you are born until you reach your teens or twenties.

From the moment you are born until you reach your teens or twenties, your body just keeps growing and growing. Your cells continue to multiply. Your bones grow longer. Your organs get bigger. This is no secret—anyone can see that you're taller, broader, and stronger than you were just a few years ago. And during all this time, your brain was growing too. You learned to speak, walk, read, count, and make friends. You discovered things that you like and things that you hate. You formed a unique personality. **Nobody out there is exactly like you.** You developed habits—some of them good, and some of them not so good. That's a lot of progress for a little more than a decade. And although it may seem hard to believe, the lifestyle choices you make now will affect you for the rest of your life. There's no better time than *now* to start forming habits that will lead to a long and healthful life. You'll be thanking yourself for that choice for many years to come.

BECOMING AN ADULT

Of course, your childhood doesn't last forever. Sometime during your early teens—or maybe earlier—everything starts to change. Your body hits puberty—the stage where it starts to become an adult body. The next few years are loaded with changes—and not all of them fun (can you say acne?). But the good news is that puberty doesn't last long. Within a few years, the body finally reaches adulthood.

After years and years of growing, your body is finally done. When you hit this stage, your cells switch over from growth mode to repair mode. Your body's task is now to keep itself in good working condition.

Soon things are changing again. Your body and its cells are aging. You may lose some strength or flexibility. You may not heal as quickly from injury. In time, you may

Acne is one unpleasant change that sometimes accompanies puberty.

begin to see gray hairs, or you may lose your hair altogether! As you reach old age, the body's cells have had a lifetime of wear and tear. Things can start to break down. Your bones may become more brittle. Your joints might hurt. You may get sick more easily.

But don't despair—aging is a part of life. And for most people, there's no reason you can't live eighty, ninety, or even one hundred years in relatively good health. Of course, a lot of that will depend on the kind of lifestyle you've chosen to lead. Think of your lifestyle choices as a sort of investment in yourself. Why not give your body and mind everything they need to grow and age in the healthiest possible way? After all, we get only one shot at this. *We might as well get it right!*

SO WHAT IS LIFESTYLE?

We're talking a lot about lifestyle. What do we mean by that? Your lifestyle is the combination of all the life choices you make, from what you eat to how much you exercise to

consequences. Poor eating choices can lead to obesity, heart disease, type 2 diabetes (a condition where the body can't properly process sugar), and other health problems. Choosing not to exercise can lead to similar results. Abusing drugs or alcohol can wreak havoc with the body and the mind.

HERE'S TO LONG LIFE!

Think about this: two thousand years ago, the average human life expectancy was in the neighborhood of twenty years. Science and medicine have only recently begun to send that figure soaring. As recently as around 1800, the average life expectancy was twenty-four. One hundred years later, it had doubled to forty-eight. By 1950 it was around seventy. And by the twenty-first century, it had climbed to over eighty.

How much further can it climb? Some scientists think we're getting close to maxing out the human life span. Others believe there's no reason a one-hundred-year life expectancy can't be a realistic goal for almost everyone.

People are living much longer than they were fifty years ago.

Too much, or too little, glucose

Insulin, a hormone that helps break down sugars and starches into glucose, is made in the pancreas in clusters of cells called the islets of Langerhans. Within the islets are alpha cells, which secrete glucagon, a hormone that regulates the level of glucose in blood, and beta cells, which secrete insulin. Insulin is released into tiny blood vessels called capillaries and carried throughout the body to be used as fuel.

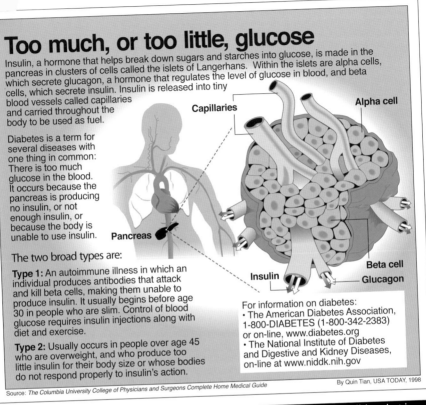

Capillaries

Alpha cell

Pancreas

Insulin

Beta cell

Glucagon

Diabetes is a term for several diseases with one thing in common: There is too much glucose in the blood. It occurs because the pancreas is producing no insulin, or not enough insulin, or because the body is unable to use insulin.

The two broad types are:

Type 1: An autoimmune illness in which an individual produces antibodies that attack and kill beta cells, making them unable to produce insulin. It usually begins before age 30 in people who are slim. Control of blood glucose requires insulin injections along with diet and exercise.

Type 2: Usually occurs in people over age 45 who are overweight, and who produce too little insulin for their body size or whose bodies do not respond properly to insulin's action.

For information on diabetes:
• The American Diabetes Association, 1-800-DIABETES (1-800-342-2383) or on-line, www.diabetes.org
• The National Institute of Diabetes and Digestive and Kidney Diseases, on-line at www.niddk.nih.gov

Source: *The Columbia University College of Physicians and Surgeons Complete Home Medical Guide*

By Quin Tian, USA TODAY, 1998

This USA TODAY excerpt gives a thorough explanation of diabetes—a condition that is closely related to diet and exercise.

There is no perfect system for how to live your life. Only you can decide what is right for you. The trick is to know that the choices are yours to make. For good or bad, you've got to be prepared to live with the consequences. Once you're ready to accept that, you're probably ready to start working toward a positive, healthful lifestyle. Keep reading for some tips on treating your body—and your mind—right.

FOR TEENS, LATER TO BED, THE WORSE THE OUTLOOK

By Greg Toppo

Teens whose parents let them stay up after midnight on weeknights have a much higher chance of being depressed or suicidal than teens whose parents enforce an earlier bedtime, says research being presented today at a national sleep conference. The findings are the first to examine bedtimes' effects on kids' mental health—and the results are noteworthy. Middle and high schoolers whose parents don't require them to be in bed before midnight on school nights are 42% more likely to be depressed than teens whose parents require a 10 P.M. or earlier bedtime. And teens who are allowed to stay up late are 30% more likely to have had suicidal thoughts in the past year. The differences are smaller but still significant—25% and 20%, respectively—after controlling for age, sex, race and ethnicity.

A team led by Columbia [New York] University Medical Center's James Gangwisch examined surveys from 15,659 teens and their parents who took part in a National Institutes of Health (NIH) adolescent health study. The survey found that kids whose parents called for a 9–10 P.M. bedtime said they were in bed, on average, by 10:04 P.M. They slept for 8 hours and 10 minutes on average, compared with 7 ½ hours for kids allowed to stay up past midnight.

Teens need about nine hours of sleep a night.

The lesson for parents is simple, Gangwisch says: try to sell teenagers on the importance of getting enough sleep. They need about nine hours, the NIH says. Rafael Pelayo, an associate professor of pediatric sleep medicine at California's Stanford University, agrees. "They've got to think it's in their own best interest to get to sleep," says Pelayo. Says Gangwisch, "We feel like we can just eat into our sleep time, but we pay for it in many different ways."

—June 9, 2009

2 DIET: IT'S NOT A *Dirty Word*

A diet is the combination of all the foods you eat. Some foods, such as apples, are more nutritious than other foods, such as ice cream.

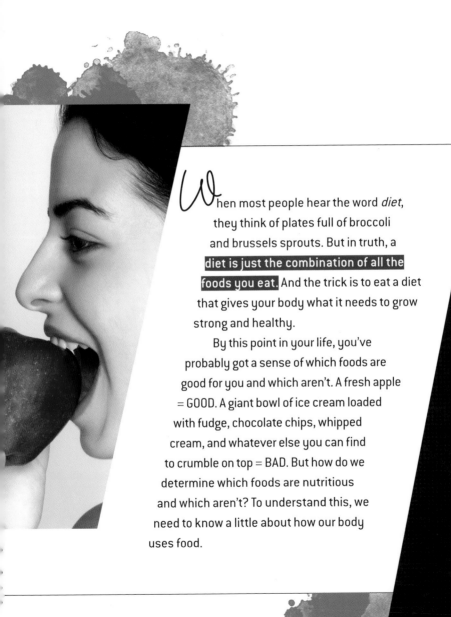

When most people hear the word *diet*, they think of plates full of broccoli and brussels sprouts. But in truth, a **diet is just the combination of all the foods you eat.** And the trick is to eat a diet that gives your body what it needs to grow strong and healthy.

By this point in your life, you've probably got a sense of which foods are good for you and which aren't. A fresh apple = GOOD. A giant bowl of ice cream loaded with fudge, chocolate chips, whipped cream, and whatever else you can find to crumble on top = BAD. But how do we determine which foods are nutritious and which aren't? To understand this, we need to know a little about how our body uses food.

Ever wake up late, skip breakfast, and rush off to school? By lunchtime, you were probably dragging. Your mind and body need energy to function, and they notice when you haven't eaten. That's because the energy you get for everything your body does—running, breathing, reading, kissing, and laughing—comes from food. Just as a car burns gasoline, your body burns through the energy stored in the food you eat.

We measure food's energy in calories. The average teenager needs between 2,000 and 2,400 calories per day, though this number depends on how active you are. You'll need more calories if you spend the whole day playing basketball than you will if you sit quietly reading all day, and boys generally need more calories than girls. If you eat too many calories, the body will store the extra energy as fat. If you don't get enough calories, the body will burn those fat stores to get the energy it needs.

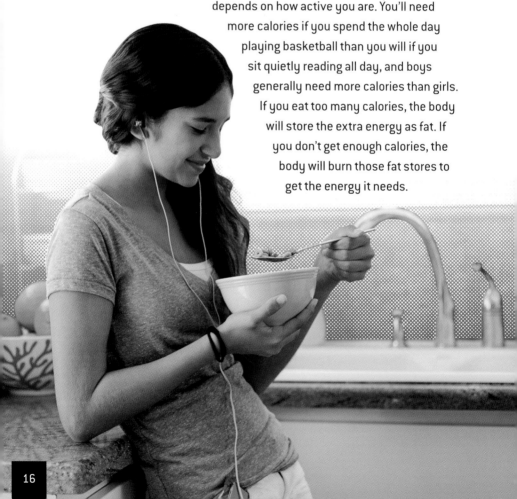

SOURCES OF ENERGY

Are all calories created equal? *Of course not!* The energy in food comes from three sources: carbohydrates (carbs), fats, and protein. Carbs are sugars and starches (starches are found in potatoes, bread, and rice). They're fairly easily converted into energy, so our bodies often crave them. Carbs come in two main types: complex and simple. Complex carbs are the best kind. Grains are loaded with complex carbs. Foods such as whole grain bread and whole grain pasta are great sources. Then there are the simple carbs—the sweet, yummy simple carbs. Sugar-loaded foods such as cookies, candy, and soda are jam-packed with simple carbs. The body can break down the simple sugars in these treats very quickly. They often provide just a quick burst of energy.

Whole grain bread is a great source of complex carbs.

USA TODAY Snapshots®

A soft drink, a burger...

Percentage of customers who ordered these items at casual restaurant chains[1]:

Carbonated soft drinks	37.5%
Burgers	12.6%
Pasta entrees	11.3%
Bagels	10.4%
Turkey club sandwich	10.0%

1 – chains that have table service, a varied menu and a full bar.
Source: NPD Group; based on year-end survey data ending February 2003

By Shannon Reilly and Sam Ward, USA TODAY, 2003

Sugary soda is a major source of simple carbs in many people's diets. This USA TODAY Snapshot shows the popularity of soft drinks at casual restaurant chains in 2003. Soft drinks remain a popular beverage choice—though plain water is more healthful.

The word *fat* may make you turn your nose up. But wait! Fat sometimes gets a bum rap. In fact, the body can't survive without it. You need some fat in your diet. The trick is finding the right kind. There are three main types of fats: unsaturated fats, saturated fats, and trans fats. Unsaturated fats are the ones you want. You can find them in foods such as fish and nuts. Saturated fats are OK in small doses as well. These fats usually come from animal products—think hamburgers, bacon, milk, and butter. But too many saturated fats can lead to health problems, including obesity and heart disease. The worst of the bunch is trans fats. These fats are made artificially. They're sometimes found in fast food or in baked goods including cookies, crackers, and even pizza crust. You should try to avoid trans fats whenever possible. Because they're not natural, your body isn't able to break them down properly. That's a bad thing.

Finally, there's protein. Proteins are made up of substances called amino acids. They're the building blocks of life. So it's no surprise that protein is among the best of all energy sources.

Almonds contain a good kind of fat—unsaturated fat.

Store-bought cupcakes can contain the worst type of fat—trans fat.

Meat is loaded with protein. Protein is one of the best energy sources.

Bodybuilders and other athletes often load up on proteins because they help build muscle and other tissues. Proteins come from meat. They're also abundant in beans, nuts, and eggs.

NUTRIENTS

Foods also give us nutrients such as vitamins and minerals. The body needs these nutrients to perform its various functions. You've probably been told to drink orange juice when you have a cold. That's because orange juice has tons of vitamin C, a nutrient that helps your body fight off diseases. Foods that are nutritious provide us with both energy and vitamins and minerals. Foods that are high in calories but low in other nutrients are often called empty calories. These are the foods to stay away from. Your body doesn't need them. So an apple = GOOD because it provides lots of nutrients as well as energy. Fudge-covered ice cream = BAD because it's mostly a big bowl of empty calories. Now if we could only convince our taste buds!

DRINK UP!

What if you could get one of the most important nutrie[nts] turning on the faucet in your kitchen sink? You can! Water [is one of] the most important parts of your diet. Water doesn't give y[ou] but the body can't function without it. You could live withou[t food for] weeks, but without water, you'd be dead in a couple of days[.]

It's OK to have a soda once in a while. But you have to r[emember] to drink clean, pure water as well. There's an easy way to tel[l if you're] getting enough water. All you have to do is look at your own u[rine.] Say what? No, it's not a joke. Next time you do your business[, take] a look. Is your urine clear or very light yellow? If so, you're pr[obably] getting enough water. Is it bright yellow? In that case, your bo[dy] almost certainly needs more water. Try an experiment. Drink a [few] glasses of water and repeat the experiment a few hours later. [See a] difference? That's your body's way of saying thanks!

of the most important [...] t. You can't survive

FILLING YOUR PLATE— HOW TO CHOOSE YOUR FOODS

All this talk about calories and nutrients is great, but you're probably wondering how it applies to real life. How are you supposed to figure out what your body needs?

The United States Department of Agriculture (USDA) wants to help. It's developed an eating guide called MyPlate. MyPlate splits food into these five food groups:

1. Grains
2. Vegetables
3. Fruits
4. Dairy
5. Protein

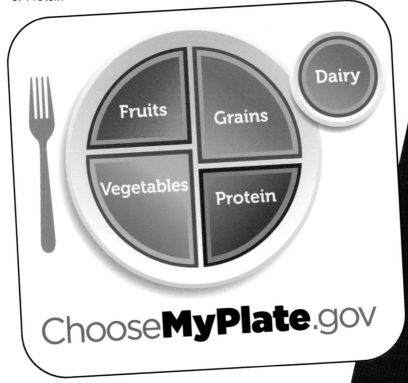

ChooseMyPlate.gov

MORE YOUNG PEOPLE GO THE VEGETARIAN ROUTE;
CHOICE BRINGS CONCERNS ABOUT PROPER NUTRITION

By Mary Brophy Marcus

Sierra pops carrot sticks and hummus the way most teens nosh on fries. Sierra, 17, of California, became a vegetarian at 13 and is among a growing number of children in the USA who are cutting meat from their diets, or at least cutting back.

There is not a glut of research and statistics on vegetarian children and their diet habits, but a [2005] poll showed that 3% of Americans ages 8 to 18 are vegetarians. That figure is up 1% from a previous poll.

Many nutrition experts say they've seen changes in the food landscape over the past 5 to 10 years that suggest a growing popularity of vegetarianism among young people. Families say it has become much less taxing to find kid-friendly vegetarian staples—such as soy milk, meat-free broths, lard-free refried beans and veggie burgers—in mainstream grocery stores. An increasing number of schools, camps and colleges have plumped their menus with more vegetarian fare, too.

Hema Sundaram, a dermatologist in Rockville, Maryland, was pleasantly surprised this spring when her 13-year-old daughter's overnight summer science camp sent a pre-camp letter offering vegetarian meal options. Sundaram says her daughter's and her 9-year-old son's school, Sidwell Friends in Washington, D.C., also provides vegetarian entrees.

The USDA urges people to eat a variety of foods from all of these groups. Focus on fruits and veggies, and make sure at least half of your grains are whole grains. Try to go for lean sources of protein, such as fish, chicken, and beans. And don't forget the dairy! Dairy products contain the mineral calcium, which your bones need to grow strong.

A growing number of children and teens are becoming vegetarians, choosing carrots and dip over chicken fingers.

Young people cite a host of reasons for going meat-free, such as personal taste, concerns about animal treatment, environmental questions surrounding livestock and the influence of peers and celebrities. [But] many non-vegetarian parents worry whether their children are getting enough nutritious food when they avoid meat.

Kaayla Daniel, a clinical nutritionist in Albuquerque, New Mexico, says, "I do think children will grow better on a high-quality omnivorous [plant- and meat-eating] diet." [However], Daniel concurs that it is possible for vegetarian children who eat fresh dairy and eggs to thrive.

"A vegetarian diet can be very healthy if it's done intelligently," says Elizabeth Turner, executive editor of Los Angeles, California-based *Vegetarian Times* magazine. "But when you cut out meat, you can't just fill that new gap on the dinner plate with carbs."

—*October 15, 2007*

ALL THINGS IN MODERATION

Not many people want to be told that they can never have ice cream, cookies, french fries, or soda. The good news is that even though these foods may be loaded with empty calories, that doesn't mean we have to cut them out entirely. *The trick is moderation.*

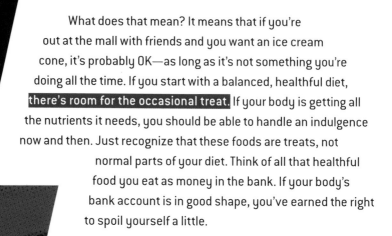

What does that mean? It means that if you're out at the mall with friends and you want an ice cream cone, it's probably OK—as long as it's not something you're doing all the time. If you start with a balanced, healthful diet, there's room for the occasional treat. If your body is getting all the nutrients it needs, you should be able to handle an indulgence now and then. Just recognize that these foods are treats, not normal parts of your diet. Think of all that healthful food you eat as money in the bank. If your body's bank account is in good shape, you've earned the right to spoil yourself a little.

If you are eating a balanced diet, it's OK to have a treat with your friends once in a while.

SIX TAKEAWAY TIPS FOR HEALTHFUL EATING

These simple takeaway tips can help you to eat more healthfully—whether you already stick to a pretty balanced diet or you're just getting started on the path to healthful eating.

- **Make half your plate fruits and veggies.** These foods are packed with nutrients that will help you look and feel your best. Orange, red, and dark green fruits and veggies are the most beneficial. Think sweet potatoes, apples, and broccoli.

- **Mix in lean protein.** Good picks include grilled chicken, beef, and pork or beans and tofu. If you like seafood, try making fish your protein source two times a week.

- **Choose whole grains.** Not sure if your favorite breads, crackers, or cereals are whole grain? Look for the label "100% whole grain" or "100% whole wheat" on the package. If they're not whole grain, try to find some foods that are. More and more whole grain options are available these days, so you're sure to find some you like!

- **Drink milk.** Skim and 1 percent milk are the best. They give you calcium without a lot of fat or calories. Soy milk is a great alternative for those who don't like cow's milk or can't drink it due to food allergies, food intolerances, or a special diet.

- **Savor your food.** Eat slowly, and pay attention to the taste and textures of what you're eating, You'll enjoy your food more, and you'll be less likely to overeat.

- **Use a smaller plate.** You may have grown up hearing that you should "clean your plate" (or eat everything on it)—but that's not always good advice. Often dinner plates are pretty big. "Cleaning" them can lead to overeating. Instead, take a smaller plate, and stop eating when you feel full. You can always take a second helping if you're still hungry after you've eaten what's on your plate.

3 SHAPE UP!: FITNESS and Exercise

It's important to be active. Participating safely in a physical activity, such as football or softball, is a great way to stay healthy.

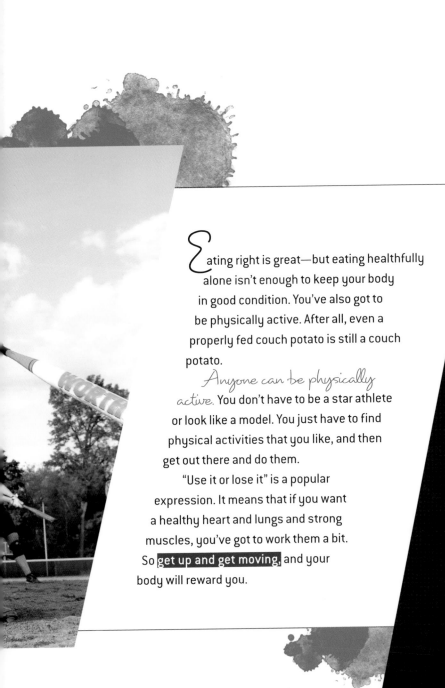

*E*ating right is great—but eating healthfully alone isn't enough to keep your body in good condition. You've also got to be physically active. After all, even a properly fed couch potato is still a couch potato.

Anyone can be physically active. You don't have to be a star athlete or look like a model. You just have to find physical activities that you like, and then get out there and do them.

"Use it or lose it" is a popular expression. It means that if you want a healthy heart and lungs and strong muscles, you've got to work them a bit. So get up and get moving, and your body will reward you.

Balance and coordination
are important to a
gymnast.

WHAT IS FITNESS?

Fitness sounds like a simple idea, but there's a lot to it. There are
many parts to fitness. These parts fall into two main categories—
skill-related fitness and health-related fitness. Skill-related
fitness refers to things such as balance, coordination, agility,
reaction time, power, and speed. These parts are important if you
want to perform well at certain activities. Suppose you want to be
a gymnast. You're probably going to need to work on your balance
and coordination. If you'd like to become a runner, speed might be
number one on your list.

Health-related fitness refers to how healthy your body is. You
want strong and flexible muscles; a steady, reliable heart; and
a body that's not overweight or too thin. Health-related fitness
breaks down into five main categories.

1. Cardiovascular fitness. Rest a finger on your neck, just under the chin and to the side of your throat. Feel that thump-thump-thumping? That's the feel of blood pulsing through your veins. Your heart is pumping all day and all night, giving all the cells in your body the blood they need to keep working. Your cardiovascular fitness is a measure of how well your heart and blood vessels work. The more active you are, the stronger your heart grows.

2. Flexibility. Do you groan every time you have to bend over to pick something up? Flexibility is how easily your joints and muscles move. If you're flexible, you can perform most body movements without too much pain or effort. The more flexible you are, the less likely you are to suffer injuries to your muscles, joints, tendons, and ligaments.

3. Muscular endurance. Ever watch the drummer in your favorite band? He or she may spend hours at a time banging away on drums while barely breaking a sweat. You need good muscular endurance to do something over and over again for a long period of time. If you get

The more flexibility you have, the less likely you are to injure yourself.

tired after five minutes of riding a bike, you'll want to work on this part of physical fitness.

4. Strength. How much weight can you lift or move? This is a measure of strength. If you've got strong muscles, you can lift a heavy backpack or open a stuck jar without any problem. You want strong, healthy muscles throughout your body—arms, legs, back, and neck.

5. Body makeup. A healthy body needs some fat—but not too much. Too much fat slows you down and places strain on your heart and lungs. But if you don't have enough fat, your body can't properly store and use its energy. You may lose body heat too quickly or be prone to illness or injury.

Figuring your body mass index

Body mass index is a measure of weight in relation to height. Anyone with a BMI of 25 or more is considered overweight. People who have a body mass index of 30 or more (a BMI of 30 is roughly 30 pounds over a healthy weight) are considered obese. BMI has some limitations: It can overestimate body fat in people who are very muscular, and it can underestimate body fat in people who have lost muscle mass, such as the elderly.

- Healthy weight
- Overweight
- Obese

Source: National Institutes of Health, 2003

Height \ Weight	120	130	140	150	160	170	180	190	200	210	220	230	240	250
4'6"	29	31	34	36	39	41	43	46	48	51	53	56	58	60
4'8"	27	29	31	34	36	38	40	43	45	47	49	52	54	56
4'10"	25	27	29	31	34	36	38	40	42	44	46	48	50	52
5'0"	23	25	27	29	31	33	35	37	39	41	43	45	47	49
5'2"	22	24	26	27	29	31	33	35	37	38	40	42	44	46
5'4"	21	22	24	26	28	29	31	33	34	36	38	40	41	43
5'6"	19	21	23	24	26	27	29	31	32	34	36	37	39	40
5'8"	18	20	21	23	24	26	27	29	30	32	34	35	37	38
5'10"	17	19	20	22	23	24	26	27	29	30	32	33	35	36
6'0"	16	18	19	20	22	23	24	26	27	28	30	31	33	34
6'2"	15	17	18	19	21	22	23	24	26	27	28	30	31	32
6'4"	15	16	17	18	20	21	22	23	24	26	27	28	29	30
6'6"	14	15	16	17	19	20	21	22	23	24	25	27	28	29
6'8"	13	14	15	17	18	19	20	21	22	23	24	25	26	28

This USA TODAY chart can give you a rough idea of whether you have a healthful body makeup. Look up your height and weight on the chart to find your body mass index (BMI). A BMI under about 18 is too low. A BMI over about 24 is too high. But keep in mind that this chart was developed mostly for adults. For a BMI calculator especially for teens, check out this website: http://apps.nccd.cdc.gov/dnpabmi/Calculator.aspx.

EXERCISE!

Want to improve your health-related fitness? It's simple—all you have to do is exercise. Some people love to exercise. Others cringe at the thought. But exercise doesn't have to be cringe-inducing. If going to the gym or running a 5k sounds like fun to you, that's great! You're probably already well on your way to being physically fit. But if these sorts of activities make you groan, don't worry—there are countless ways to give your body the activity it needs.

The first step in developing good exercise habits is to **figure out what you enjoy.** Don't like running or lifting weights? No problem. Maybe an afternoon playing basketball or tennis sounds like more fun. Perhaps you like long, leisurely walks or bike rides. Or maybe you love to dance. These activities are great exercise. Focusing on activities you enjoy is the key to keeping up your fitness. And get your exercise at the time of day when you feel energetic and motivated. You might be able to drag yourself out of bed early to jog every day for a week or two. But if you truly don't enjoy doing it, you probably won't be able to keep it up.

Taking a long, leisurely walk with a friend is a great way to get some exercise.

designed to offer physical, mental, and spiritual benefits. It stresses flexibility, endurance, and self-control. Although many find it to be a very peaceful activity, yoga can also provide a great workout.

The best part about yoga is that virtually anyone of any fitness level can do it. If you're interested in trying it out, check out a yoga book or DVD (your local library might have some) or hit the Net to look for classes. Many instructors offer free introductory classes, especially in large cities. Some classes are even tailored specifically to teens.

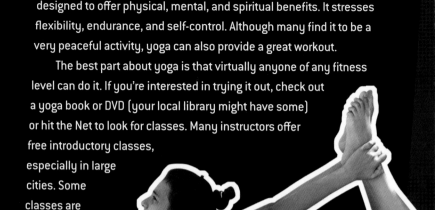

Sometimes it's hard to find the time to exercise. Your schoolwork may be weighing you down. After-school activities might be eating into what little spare time you have. Or maybe you've got a job that takes up a lot of your time. You can still find ways to move your body. Take the stairs instead of using an escalator or an elevator. Maybe you can walk or ride your bike to school or work instead of getting a ride.

Instead of sitting in a chair in front of your computer, you might try sitting on an exercise ball.

If you have to sit in front of a computer doing homework, you might try sitting on an exercise ball instead of a chair. This forces your abdominal (stomach) muscles, back muscles, and leg muscles to work even while you're just sitting there! Whatever the situation, try to find some way to get your blood pumping. Then, when you do get the time for some full-on exercise, use it! Nobody ever got physically fit by plopping down on the couch and watching TV. If you feel your motivation starting to dip, remember that exercising will help you feel better about yourself and *look* better. You'll have better muscle tone and a more fit physique. And who doesn't want to look their best?

Making exercise a habit is a big part of leading a healthful lifestyle. Before long, you won't even have to think about it or force yourself to do it. Your body will crave the exercise, and you'll want that feeling that comes with working up a good sweat. When you exercise, your brain releases chemicals called endorphins. Endorphins activate the pleasure centers of your brain. Once you get used to that endorphin rush, your mind and body will beg you for more. Exercise is one of the few addictions in life that's actually good for you!

USA TODAY
Life
SECTION D
LIFE.USATODAY.COM

MOTIVATED FAMILIES CAN MAKE FITNESS A GOAL FOR ALL

By Nanci Hellmich

Only a third of Americans meet the government's guidelines for physical activity, which are at least 2½ hours a week of moderate-intensity activity (such as brisk walking) for adults and one hour a day for children and teens. To help families get in better shape, USA TODAY is challenging families to try some new activities together every week for eight weeks. You can repeat the ones you really like or give them all a try.

Week 1: Take an active staycation day.

Work with your family to plan a one-day active staycation—a low-cost vacation day near home. Make it a day of physical activities: Go on a hike at a nearby park or through a city you've wanted to explore.

Week 2: Stage a sports competition.

Split the family into two teams and host a day of friendly competition in several games and sports—table tennis, relay races, basketball, [and] swimming are a few to try.

Week 3: Go retro active.

Spend an hour every night for one week doing an old-fashioned physical activity together that someone in the family has never done before. Consider Hula-Hooping or playing games such as hopscotch, Simon Says, hide-and-seek, and four square.

Week 4: Give dance a chance.

Figure out a dance the entire family can learn and practice it all week. It might be the waltz, line dancing, foxtrot or salsa. If no one knows how to dance, rent a DVD that will give you some guidance. Have fun and put on a show at the end. Make a video of the show.

Try new activities with your family, such as Hula-Hooping or jumping rope, to help you get in shape.

Week 5: Set the stage for fun and games.

Put together an activity area and then spend an hour or longer each day for a week there. Gather some simple, inexpensive toys and sports equipment that the family can use to play outdoors.

Week 6: Go on an active scavenger hunt.

Plan a one- to two-hour scavenger hunt. You can explore a nearby park, your home, the woods, the mall—even the grocery store. At the supermarket, each family member might pick a different color fruit or veggie, find a yogurt that's low in sugar (10 to 15 grams), or find a bread that lists 100% whole wheat as a main ingredient.

Week 7: Indulge your inner child with a play date.

Go to a nearby park or playground and become a kid again: Climb on the monkey bars, slide down the slide, and see how high and long you can glide on the swings. The entire family has to give it a go.

Week 8: Go camping.

This can be an overnight trip or a day trip in your backyard or on your deck or even inside the house. [Families with] young children . . . can make tents out of blankets and card tables in [the] living room. [Families with] older children . . . might plan a trip to a nearby state park.

—*June 28, 2010*

4 STAY CLEAN: SUBSTANCES *and Abuse*

Substances such as alcohol and caffeine can affect how your mind and body work.

$\mathcal{W}$e've talked about how diet and physical activity impact your lifestyle. But the story doesn't end there. To lead a healthful life, you've also got to be **smart about substances.** Think alcohol, tobacco, drugs, and even caffeine. Substances affect how your brain and body work—and sometimes, substances can be very dangerous.

DANGER!

What exactly makes a substance dangerous? In truth, almost any substance in excess can be harmful to the body. Think of something as simple as aspirin. This drug can help you deal with pain, reduce swelling, and even help you avoid heart disease. In small doses, it can be very good for you. But too much of it causes all kinds of problems. It can chew through the lining of your stomach. It can result in poisoning, which causes nausea, vomiting, and dizziness and can even lead to death! It's just one example of why many substances are good in moderation but very bad in excess.

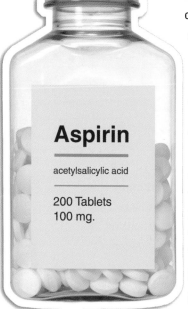

Of course, many substances bring just the danger with none of the benefits. Have you ever been offered alcohol, tobacco, or drugs? If so, did you spend much time thinking about what these substances do to your body? Parents, teachers, and other responsible adults have probably told you to steer clear of these substances and for good reason. They're the fast track to an unhealthful lifestyle. They put all sorts of strains on your body and mind.

ALCOHOL: BE AWARE

You probably see alcohol all around you. Advertisements for beer, wine, and hard liquor are everywhere. You may even see these items in your local grocery store. Maybe your parents drink alcohol. So why is it so bad for you?

To understand why, you need a handle on what alcohol does to the body. Alcohol is a depressant. This means that it slows brain function. It even blocks some of the signals to the brain.

Alcohol can be seen in advertisements and on display at the grocery store. But alcohol kills brain cells and slows brain function.

You've probably seen people who were intoxicated—or drunk—on alcohol, either in person or on TV. They often stagger, slur their speech, and have emotional outbursts. Their judgment is impaired and their reaction times are slowed (these are the main reasons that driving drunk is so dangerous). Alcohol also kills brain cells. And trust us: you want to hold onto as many of those as you can!

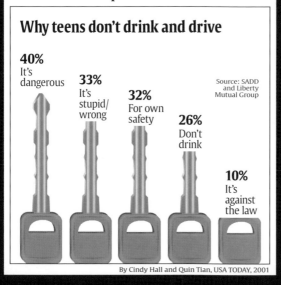

Source: SADD and Liberty Mutual Group

USA TODAY Snapshots®

Why teens don't drink and drive

40%
It's dangerous

33%
It's stupid/ wrong

32%
For own safety

26%
Don't drink

10%
It's against the law

By Cindy Hall and Quin Tian, USA TODAY, 2001

Most teens know that drinking and driving don't mix. This USA TODAY Snapshot shows the reasons teens give for why they don't drink and drive.

Alcohol can be hard on the body as well. Teen drinkers are more likely to be overweight. They can suffer from high blood pressure. Drinking also can damage the liver. Prolonged drinking can lead to alcoholism, or addiction to alcohol. Alcoholism is serious business. It's a condition that can ruin lives and break up families.

And of course, the slow reaction time and impaired judgment that comes with drinking leads to **many more injuries and deaths.** Car accidents and domestic violence (violence within a household or in a family) both often increase when alcohol is involved.

THE TROUBLE WITH TOBACCO

It's no secret that tobacco is bad for you—but you may not know just how bad it is for you. In any form, tobacco contains chemicals that are both addictive and cancer-causing. Cigarettes contain nicotine, tar, carbon monoxide, and other nasty chemicals. As a smoker draws smoke into his or her lungs, these chemicals come along for the ride.

IT'S NOT JUST DRUGS!

When you think of substances that are harmful to your health, alcohol, tobacco, and drugs probably come to mind right away. But they aren't the only substances that can harm you. Sunlight can cause skin cancer if you get too much of it. Eating badly charred food can lead to problems in the stomach and intestines. And pesticides and herbicides (chemicals used to kill insects and weeds in fields of crops) can get onto foods and into your body.

You can't avoid every harmful substance out there. But by staying aware of your environment and of what you're eating and drinking, you can minimize the danger. You can wear sunblock if you're going to be spending time in the sun. If you burn your burger on the grill, cut away the charred parts. You can limit your exposure to insect- and weed-killing chemicals by eating organic foods. These are foods that have been grown without chemical pesticides and herbicides. Especially look for organic peaches, apples, grapes, and bell peppers. People often eat the skins of these foods, and the skins are where most of the pesticides and herbicides accumulate. On the other hand, it's usually fine to eat conventionally grown bananas, pineapples, and avocados. That's good news, since organic foods usually cost a little more than conventionally grown foods.

Sunlight can cause skin cancer, so it's important to wear sunblock when you spend time in the sun.

Over time, they build up. Check out the photo of a smoker's lungs below. Not pretty, is it?

Of course, cigarettes aren't the only form of tobacco. Chewing tobacco can be just as bad. But instead of delivering cancer-causing chemicals to your lungs, chewing tobacco delivers them to your mouth, throat, and stomach. You think stomach cancer sounds like fun? Yeah, not so much. The same is true for cigars.

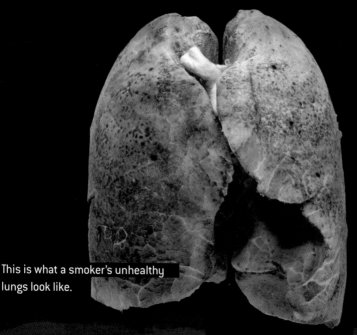

This is what a smoker's unhealthy lungs look like.

Like cigarettes, cigars are smoked. They don't contain as many chemicals, and most people don't inhale cigar smoke deep into their lungs, but the smoke can wreak havoc with the mouth and throat. In truth, there's no safe form of tobacco. All forms are potentially deadly and all terribly addictive. The best defense against tobacco addiction is to never even try tobacco products.

And if the negative consequences to your health don't convince you to avoid tobacco, consider this: *Tobacco is really, really expensive!* The average cigarette smoker can easily spend $150 per month on cigarettes. That's a lot of green just going up in smoke. Think of all the other ways you could spend that money. Heck, for just a month's worth of cigarettes, you could snag a nice new MP3 player, a leather jacket, or some primo seats to a concert. Add it up over the course of a few years, and you're talking about a set of wheels, a top-of-the-line computer, or even a nice chunk of your college education.

ILLEGAL DRUGS: NOT WORTH THE RISK

From marijuana to cocaine to heroin to crystal meth, illegal drugs can be a quick ticket to addiction, overdose, a criminal record, and even death. That's a whole lot of bad without any real good. When you think about it, drug use just doesn't make any sense. No amount of peer pressure in the world should be enough to convince you to throw your life away.

Unlike alcohol and tobacco, illegal drugs are completely unregulated. What does that mean? It means that no government or business agency makes sure they're made properly. So even if a friend assures you that a drug is safe, you can never know. **All it takes is one bad batch to bring your life to a tragic halt.** *Just say no* may sound like a cliché, but it's still the best advice you can take.

PRESCRIPTION DRUGS— A HIDDEN DANGER

If illegal drugs are unsafe, that must mean that prescription drugs are perfectly OK, right? *Wrong!* Prescription drugs can be every bit as dangerous as the hardest of illegal drugs. That's why you should use them only under a doctor's orders. A doctor understands the dangers and knows the exact dosage your body can handle.

Using drugs that aren't prescribed to you can lead to addiction or overdoses. It can damage organs including your liver and kidneys. Take too much of a drug or take drugs in the wrong combination and it could kill you. Don't fool yourself into believing that just because the drugs come with fancy labels and in neat, official-looking packages, they must be safe to take. Any time you're popping a pill that wasn't prescribed for you, you're rolling the dice. Is your health and life really worth the risk?

OVERCOMING ADDICTION

What do you do if you or someone you love is addicted to a dangerous substance? A good first step is to talk about the problem. If it's a friend or a family member, lend a supportive ear and tell the person you'll do what you can to help him or her quit. If it's you who has the problem, find someone you trust and talk about it. Addiction may be a hard problem to admit to, especially to a parent. But telling someone may be your best move, no matter how scary or embarrassing the idea seems. If you don't think you can talk to a parent or if your parent has the problem, find help elsewhere. A member of the clergy may be able to lend a sympathetic ear. A favorite teacher, a school counselor, or even a friend's parent might be able to help.

In severe cases, the support of friends and family members may not be enough. You might need more help. Programs such as Alcoholics Anonymous help people overcome addictions. So do rehabilitation centers. Going to a rehab center may not sound like a lot of fun, but if that's what it takes to overcome an addiction, it will be well worth it. Always remember that the goal is to get healthy and lead the sort of lifestyle that will allow you to stay that way. If that takes a little short-term pain, it's time to grit your teeth and get on with it. If you can do what it takes, you'll soon be back to living a clean, healthful lifestyle that will have you feeling better.

PRESCRIPTION DRUGS
FIND PLACE IN TEEN CULTURE

Donna Leinwand

When a teenager in Jan Sigerson's office mentioned a "pharm party" in February, Sigerson thought the youth was talking about a keg party out on a farm. "Pharm," it turned out, was short for pharmaceuticals [prescription drugs]. Sigerson, program director for Journeys, a teen drug treatment program in Omaha, Nebraska, soon learned that area youths were organizing parties to down fistfuls of prescription drugs.

Experts say prescription pills have become popular among youths because they are easy to get and represent a more socially acceptable way of getting high than taking street drugs. And some kids [are believed to be] self-medicating undiagnosed depression or anxiety.

Lisa Cappiello, 39, of Brooklyn, New York, says that seemed to be the case with her son, Eddie. She knew that he had tried marijuana at 15 and sneaked beers at school. But it wasn't until after he graduated from high school and took a year off before college that Cappiello realized the extent of her son's drug use—and the hold prescription drugs had on him. "In what seemed like the blink of an eye, it went from marijuana and an occasional beer to so much Xanax that [one day] my husband had to pick him up when he fell asleep on a street corner waiting for some friends," she said. The next day, Eddie Cappiello admitted to his parents that he had taken 15 pills of Xanax. He told his parents Xanax helped him deal with anxiety and depression.

Eddie rejected professional help and vowed to stop taking pills, his mother says. He was clean for 10 months before he was hospitalized in July 2005 after overdosing. Two months later, he entered a 28-day treatment program. After he was discharged, he stayed clean for about two months—then relapsed into weekend binging: 40 to 50 pills and a quart of Jack Daniel's, sometimes by himself, sometimes with friends.

Eddie Cappiello, 22, died in his bed on Feb. 17 after overdosing on a mix of pharmaceuticals. "Before four years ago, I never even heard the word *Xanax*," Lisa Cappiello says. "Now . . . I know kids as young as 12 are using it."

—June 13, 2006

5 PEACE OF MIND:
Emotional Health

The health of your mind is intertwined with the health of your body. It's important to take care of both.

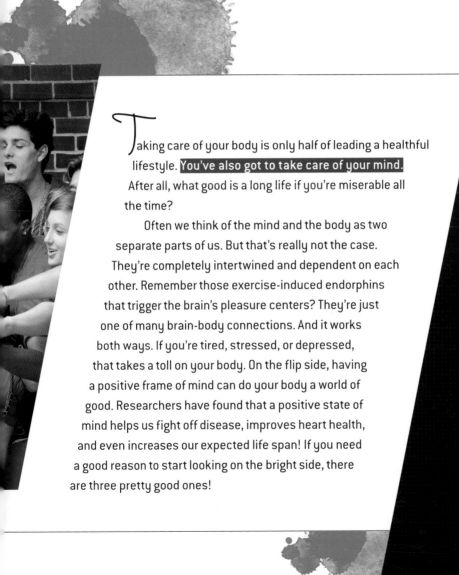

Taking care of your body is only half of leading a healthful lifestyle. You've also got to take care of your mind. After all, what good is a long life if you're miserable all the time?

Often we think of the mind and the body as two separate parts of us. But that's really not the case. They're completely intertwined and dependent on each other. Remember those exercise-induced endorphins that trigger the brain's pleasure centers? They're just one of many brain-body connections. And it works both ways. If you're tired, stressed, or depressed, that takes a toll on your body. On the flip side, having a positive frame of mind can do your body a world of good. Researchers have found that a positive state of mind helps us fight off disease, improves heart health, and even increases our expected life span! If you need a good reason to start looking on the bright side, there are three pretty good ones!

Of course, keeping a positive outlook isn't always as simple as snapping your fingers and thinking happy thoughts (though that doesn't hurt!). Keep reading to learn more about how to give your brain what it needs to survive and thrive.

USA TODAY Snapshots®

Why kids eat
American children ages, 8-17, say they eat all or most of the time when they feel:

Hungry — 77%

Bored — 14%

Angry or depressed — 6%

Source: Pursuant Inc. for American Dietetic Association Foundation

By Marisa Navarro and Marcy E. Mullins, USA TODAY, 2003

...y-mind connection can create a vicious cycle. Sometimes people turn to food ...ey feel bad—and overeating to fight bad feelings can make people feel worse. ...JSA TODAY Snapshot shows, about 20 percent of kids ages eight to seventeen ...n they feel bored, angry, or depressed.

SLEEP: IT'S NOT WASTED TIME!

Sleep—it's that familiar activity that each of us spends about a third of our lives doing. Sometimes, that might seem like a royal waste of time. Think of all you could get done with another eight or nine hours each day!

But sleep is anything but a waste of time. It's a critical part of your physical and mental health. Over the course of a day, your brain and body take in a ton of information. They're constantly working to process everything they see, hear, smell, taste, and touch. That's a lot of work! You might think that sleep is the brain's way of shutting itself off for a bit. But that's actually not the case. The brain simply switches gears and gets to work on sorting through all the information we've taken in (that's probably why babies sleep so much more than adults— they've got a lot of new info to process!). Some scientists think that during sleep, the brain forms long-term memories. It may also be hard at work on some heavy-duty problem solving. Ever hear somebody say that they want to "sleep on it" when facing a big decision? It's actually a good idea. While you're snoring away, your brain is making connections and helping you to see the problem more clearly.

When you're not getting enough sleep, your brain isn't getting the time it needs to do all this behind-the-scenes work. It won't take long before you start seeing the effects. Your ability to make decisions will degrade. You'll become forgetful. Your emotions may start running out of control. You'll be cranky and irritable. You may become easily stressed. As a result, your immune system (the parts of your body that fight off disease) will be weakened, and you'll be more likely to

If you don't get enough sleep, you can become cranky and irritable.

get sick. In short, you won't be a ton of fun to be around, and you'll be less able to learn and process information. These are all bad things!

So how much sleep do you need? Many health experts suggest that nine hours a night is about right for teenagers. And it's best to get this sleep on a regular schedule. You may feel you're too old to have a "bedtime," but in truth, it's not a bad thing. Getting quality, regular sleep is likely to keep you happier, sharper, and more ready to deal with whatever life has to throw at you.

STRESS!

Homework piling up, friends pulling you in different directions, problems at home . . . sometimes it might seem as if your life is becoming more and more stressful by the day. But believe it or not, stress isn't always bad. It's all a question of how much stress we have and how we deal with it.

Piles of homework that are due the next day can put stress on your body. But not all forms of stress are bad.

What is stress, and what's the point of it? Stress is your body's reaction to the demands of the world. There are two main types of stress. The first is acute stress. Acute stress is usually short and powerful. Imagine that you're walking home from school. As you round a corner, a big, strange, snarling dog comes charging toward you. Bam—instant stress! Your body reacts immediately with a response called flight-or-fight. Your muscles tense, and a chemical called adrenaline surges into your bloodstream. The body is preparing to either defend itself or run away. Of course, acute stress isn't just for life-or-death situations. Asking a boy or girl out for the first time can create acute stress. So can a pop quiz at school or a minor car accident. In all these cases, the body reacts to deal with a short-term situation. There's really nothing wrong with a little acute stress in your life.

Chronic stress is another sort of beast. This is stress that sticks around for a long time. It might happen if a parent is out of work and the family is having money problems. Or if a kid is constantly living in fear of being bullied. The body reacts to long-term stress much as it does to acute stress. But the problem is that we're not built to be under such constant stress. It's bad for your body as well as your state of mind. Chronic stress can lead to stomach ulcers (sores in the lining of the stomach), headaches, and sleep problems.

DEAL WITH IT

We can't get rid of stress. There's always going to be something to worry about. **The trick is learning to manage stress.** Some people have a natural knack for letting worries roll off them. They take an attitude that they'll control what they can and not spend too much time worrying about what they can't. For others, this kind of carefree attitude doesn't come as naturally.

GEN NEXTERS
HAVE THEIR HANDS FULL

By Sharon Jayson

Seventeen-year-old Alex hopes his senior year of high school will be less stressful than his junior year. "It was a pretty overwhelming workload," he says. Besides taking two Advanced Placement classes, honors chemistry, math and electives, he served on the student council organizing community service projects, took a cultural diversity class at a community college for college credit, participated in his school's alcohol awareness group, did volunteer work, took tennis lessons and held down a part-time job.

For Alex's generation, "overwhelming" is par for the course. And those who study teens and people in their early 20s say young people are plenty stressed out. They're coming of age in a globally competitive world where the path to the middle class is no longer a high school diploma. More students go to college; it's also costly and more selective, and they know it can change their lives. The particulars vary, but young people from all walks of life are feeling the strain.

"What contemporary American culture advertises is achievement and accomplishment as the route to ultimate happiness," says Suniya Luthar, a professor of psychology and education at Columbia University in New York. She has spent much of the past decade studying affluent young people. Luthar and others say a host of factors have resulted in an especially anxiety-prone

But never fear. If you tend to worry, you can take steps to reduce the toll that stress takes on you. Exercise—moving your body and spending some of that pent-up energy—can be a great kind of therapy. Another way to deal with stress is to *try some simple relaxation tactics.* Find a quiet moment in your day. Close your eyes and block everything out. Breathe deeply through your nose. Then slowly exhale

generation, dealing with not just a faster-paced, technology-dominated society but also with their own lofty aspirations and their parents' expectations.

Data show that more young people are diagnosed with mental health problems, but Luanne Southern of the National Mental Health Association says the increase could be attributable to greater public awareness about mental health. A study by psychologists at Kansas State University published three years ago found that the number of college-age students treated for depression doubled from 1989 to 2001. And the University of Michigan Depression Center estimates that as many as 15% of college students are depressed.

Psychologist Sherry Benton, assistant director of the counseling service at Kansas State University, studies student mental health. The higher a student's grade point average, the more likely he or she is to seek help, Benton says. More than half of the center's clients have GPAs of 3.2 or better. "They do pretty well and think 'I can take on a little more,'" she says. "They're afraid they'll lose their edge." They think they can get by with a little less sleep. Pretty soon they're skipping meals. They don't exercise. They have no recovery time. It's all stress. Run, run, run."

Alex is still working to improve his college prospects by boosting his standardized test scores. He has already taken the ACT "a couple of times," and "I think I'll take it again to see if my score will go up a little more." He also took the SAT and says he might take it again, too.

—*August 21, 2006*

through your mouth. Let your breath just sort of slowly flow out of you. Imagine that your breath contains all your stress and worries. That stress is flowing out of your body as you slowly exhale. Some people find that it helps to imagine the stress as a color. Imagine clouds of that color leaving your body as you're breathing out.

If that doesn't do the trick, try some simple meditation. Find a quiet place where you can comfortably sit or lie still. Imagine a place where you feel safe. It could be your bedroom, your backyard, or a warm beach on a desert island—wherever you feel at peace. Allow your mind to go to that place. Imagine the sights, sounds, and smells of it. If you're at a beach, listen to the ocean waves crashing in and smell the salty air. If you're in your backyard, hear the birds chirping. Spend a few moments in your safe place. When you open your eyes, you might find yourself recharged and ready to face the world.

Of course, these techniques don't actually remove the stress. They just *help your body relax a bit*. If the stress in your life is getting to be more than you can handle, you need to talk to someone about it. Start with a parent, a teacher, or a school counselor. If that doesn't help—or if you don't feel comfortable talking to any of these people—it may be time to consider seeing a therapist or a psychologist. These professionals can give you more advanced strategies for relaxing and dealing with stress.

...ion in a quiet place can help you feel ...e and relax your body.

SEXUAL HEALTH

So by the time you're a teenager, you've probably noticed a whole new source of stress in your life—*sex!* Suddenly, boys or girls might have an appeal that they didn't when you were a kid. You may find yourself thinking a lot about romantic relationships and sexual activity. Nothing's wrong with having these sorts of thoughts. It's natural. You've just got to remember that sex is serious business with big-time consequences. Are you prepared to become a parent or to get a sexually transmitted disease that you'll carry through the rest of your life? Probably not!

The attitudes you have about sex are affected by a lot of different factors—religion, culture, family life, your peer group, and more. What's important to remember is that any choices you make about this part of your life have to be *your* choices. Don't let friends, boyfriends, or girlfriends push you into doing things that you're not ready to do—and be sure to protect yourself. Understand the consequences of sex, both emotionally and physically. Don't be afraid to ask your parents or other trusted adults about sex. It may be hard to believe, but they were your age once. They may be willing to share their wisdom.

The decision about whether to have sex is your choice. Don't let anyone push you into something you are not ready for.

Happiness, sadness, fear, anger, and excitement—emotions are a big part of who we are. Even negative emotions have their place. For example, if a beloved pet dies, you're supposed to be sad. It's part of the grieving process. Likewise, a little anxiety before a first date is natural. The important part about emotions is making sure we control them, not the other way around.

Have you ever spent time with toddlers? When they're happy, they're almost delirious. When they're sad, they seem to be in a pit of utter despair. If they're angry, they fly off the handle in a fit of pure rage. Their emotions can jump all over the place in a very short time span. This is because toddlers haven't gained much emotional maturity. They haven't learned to control their emotions at all. Luckily, most teenagers and adults have come a long way since then. You know how to control your emotions, at least somewhat. You can face your fears. Your highs aren't as high, and your lows aren't as low— or at least you know not to throw yourself on the floor kicking and screaming when you *do* hit a really low point! But even as you get older, emotions can pose some real problems.

One of the most widespread emotional problems is depression. Everyone gets a little depressed now and then. Maybe it just seems as if everything is going against you. Or maybe you've had a nasty fight with a friend or a family member. As long as the depression passes, it's probably not a big deal. But for some people, intense feelings of sadness just won't go away. These people may even feel sad when nothing apparent is wrong. This is when depression becomes a problem. People who are depressed

Depression is one of the most widespread mental illnesses.

often lack drive to do anything. The stress of depression can be harmful to their health. In extreme cases, depression can drive people to drastic acts such as cutting themselves on purpose or even committing suicide.

Most people can get through minor bouts of depression on their own. **A good night's sleep can be a huge help.** So can some exercise (endorphins are great natural antidepressants!). Sometimes talking about things is a big help. You can talk to a sibling, a parent, or a friend. At school, a teacher or a school counselor might be able to lend a sympathetic ear. Heck, even talking to a pet can help. They may not offer much advice, but they're great listeners!

Sadness isn't the only emotion that can run amok. Some people struggle to control other emotions, such as anxiety and anger. Someone with an anxiety disorder may feel fearful or intensely nervous about everyday situations. Maybe the idea of talking to strangers is too scary to even think about. Or maybe even the sight of a dog inspires panic—even if it's a familiar dog, and it's friendly and wearing a leash.

People who struggle to control their anger may lash out at others over small disagreements. They may shout or curse rather than dealing with problems in a productive way. Just as with depression, talking about these problems can be a big help. Sometimes all you need to do is get some things off your chest to feel a lot better and more at peace.

If any of these problems persist, it might be time to consider professional help. A trained therapist or psychologist can help you confront and deal with the emotions that are causing the trouble. Just remember: The first step in overcoming any of these conditions is to **recognize the problem and ask for help.** If admitting a problem seems a little embarrassing, it may help to remember that you'll be doing yourself and the people who love you a big favor by getting yourself in a healthful state of mind.

CHOOSING *Health*

Staying in the habit of exercising and eating right will help keep your mind and body healthy.

Keeping up a healthful lifestyle might sound complicated, but it's really not too hard. By now, you've got a pretty good sense of what's good for you and what isn't. It's no big secret that a plate of grilled chicken and veggies is more healthful for you than eating half of a greasy pizza. And you surely know that going out to play some flag football with friends is better for you than plopping down in front of the TV to veg out. Really, it's not rocket science.

So then why is leading a healthful lifestyle so hard for so many people? Consider one simple word: *habit.* People are creatures of habit. Most of us like routine. We get used to what we know, and we're comfortable with that. When our habits are harmful to our health, that's a problem. Changing bad habits can be a difficult and even painful process.

But there's good news here too: good habits are just as powerful as bad ones! If you get into the habit of exercising, you'll find yourself craving that physical activity. The same is true with food. Once you make a habit out of giving your body the right kind of fuel, you'll find it's easy. It's true across the board—even something such as keeping a positive mental outlook can become a habit.

We can't control everything when it comes to our health, but there's a lot we can do. And the best part is that, for the most part, you already know what's good for you and what's bad. *It's mostly a matter of willpower.* Do you have what it takes to turn down a second piece of cake at a party or have a glass of water instead of a soda? Are you willing to peel yourself off the couch to take a walk, lift some weights, or do some yoga? Will you choose to go outside and shoot baskets instead of playing a basketball video game? Can you say no to using drugs, alcohol, tobacco, or other harmful substances, even if your friends are doing it? If you think about it this way, you realize that leading a healthful lifestyle doesn't require you to read medical journals and study nutrition guides. All you've got to do is apply some common sense to the decisions you make every day. It's all about the choices you make, and nobody controls that but you.

So what will you choose? There's no better time than *now* to make the life changes that will give you decades of health and well-being.

GLOSSARY

ADRENALINE: a hormone (chemical) that is released by the adrenal gland in response to stress. Adrenaline is also called epinephrine. It prepares the body for the fight-or-flight response.

AMINO ACID: the basic building block of a cell

CALORIE: a measurement of the amount of energy a food gives you

CARBOHYDRATE: a nutrient found in sugars and starches

DEPRESSION: a condition of mental disturbance, often with the feeling of long-lasting or profound sadness. Depression often leads to a lack of energy and difficulty in maintaining concentration or interest in life.

DIET: the combination of all the foods you eat

ENDORPHIN: a hormone released by the brain in response to exercise and other stimuli. Endorphins often promote a sense of pleasure and well-being.

LIFESTYLE: the way in which a person lives, including choices about food, exercise, sexuality, and more

MEDITATION: a practice through which one creates a mode of relaxed and open consciousness, often resulting in a feeling of peace. Meditation can have very positive effects on both mental and physical health.

NICOTINE: a chemical found in tobacco that works as a stimulant and is highly addictive

NUTRIENT: a healthful substance found in food

OBESITY: a condition in which a person has excessive body fat

PROTEIN: a nutrient made of amino acids. Protein helps build bones and muscles.

STRESS: a physical, chemical, or emotional factor that causes bodily or mental tension

TYPE 2 DIABETES: a condition in which the body is unable to properly process sugar. Type 2 diabetes is often caused by unhealthful eating choices. Another type of diabetes, type 1, also makes the body unable to properly process sugar, but it isn't caused by unhealthful eating. Genetics and exposure to certain viruses may cause type 1.

SELECTED BIBLIOGRAPHY

Corbin, Charles B., and Ruth Lindsey. *Fitness for Life.* Champaign, IL: Human Kinetics, 2007.

Ditson, Mary, Caesar Pacifici, and Lee White. *The Teenage Human Body: Operator's Manual.* Eugene, OR: Northwest Media, 1998.

Mazel, Judy, and John E. Monaco. *Slim & Fit Kids: Raising Healthy Children in a Fast-Food World.* Deerfield Beach, FL: Health Communications,1999.

Nemours Foundation. *TeensHealth.* 2011. http://kidshealth.org/teen (July 13, 2011).

Parker, Gordon. *Dealing with Depression: A Commonsense Guide to Mood Disorders.* Crows Nest, Australia: Allen & Unwin, 2002.

Stitt, Allan. *Mediation: A Practical Guide.* Portland, OR: Cavendish, 2004.

USDA. choosemyplate.gov. N.d. http://www.choosemyplate.gov/ (July 13, 2011).

Willett, Walter C. *Eat, Drink, and Be Healthy: The Harvard Medical School Guide to Healthy Eating.* New York: Free Press, 2005.

FURTHER INFORMATION

Bingham, Jane. *Stress and Depression.* Pleasantville, NY: Gareth Stevens, 2009.
  This book takes a hard look at the role of stress in depression, offers coping
  tips, and suggests ways that teens can seek help.

Canino, Kate. *Maintaining a Healthy Weight.* New York: Rosen Central, 2011.
  Keeping your body at a healthful weight—not too low and not too high—is a
  big part of staying healthy. Learn more about what a healthful body weight
  is and how to get there—and *stay* there.

ChooseMyPlate
  http://www.choosemyplate.gov
  Check out this page to learn more about MyPlate—the USDA's guide to
  healthful eating.

Doeden, Matt. *Eat Right!: How You Can Make Good Food Choices.* Minneapolis:
  Lerner Publications Company, 2009.
  Discover more about how the body uses and processes food, and find
  strategies for building a healthful diet.

———. *Stay Fit!: How You Can Get in Shape.* Minneapolis: Lerner Publications
  Company, 2009.
  Learn how physical activity impacts the body and how to test your own
  level of physical fitness.

Foundation for a Drug-Free World
  http://www.drugfreeworld.org/home.html
  The home page for the Foundation for a Drug-Free World provides a wealth
  of information on drugs and addiction. This teen-friendly site offers
  testimonials from those who have beaten addiction and offers tips on
  helping a friend quit.

Hunt, Jamie. *Getting Stronger, Getting Fit: The Importance of Exercise.* Broomall,
  PA: Mason Crest Publishers, 2010.
  Hunt explores the problem of obesity among young people and offers tips
  on ways readers can exercise and get fit.

It's My Life
http://pbskids.org/itsmylife
This website features useful information on a variety of health-related issues, from eating and nutrition to physical fitness.

Medina, Sarah. *Know the Facts about Drugs*. New York: Rosen Central, 2010.
Read about drugs—from alcohol to steroids to cocaine and heroin—and learn how they affect the mind and body. This book offers tips on making the right choices and helping a friend who is struggling with substance abuse.

Sex, Etc.
http://www.sexetc.org
This site is devoted to sex education for teens. It's got info on dating, birth control, sexually transmitted diseases, pregnancy, and much more.

Teens and Sleep
http://www.sleepfoundation.org/article/sleep-topics/teens-and-sleep
This article from the National Sleep Foundation is about sleep and why it's so important.

TeensHealth
http://kidshealth.org/teen
This site is loaded with information about your health, ranging from nutrition and exercise to diseases to sexuality.

Yancey, Diane. *STDs*. Minneapolis: Twenty-First Century Books, 2012.
Yancey discusses sexually transmitted diseases and why practicing safe sex is crucial to your health.

LERNER

SOURCE

Expand learning beyond the printed book. Download free, complementary educational resources for this book from our website, www.lerneresource.com.

INDEX

ABOUT THE AUTHOR

Matt Doeden is a writer and editor who lives in New Prague, Minnesota. After earning degrees in journalism and psychology from Minnesota State University–Mankato, he began his career as a sportswriter. Since then, he's spent nearly a decade writing and editing nonfiction on topics that range from extreme sports to military equipment to health and self-care. In addition to this title, he authored *Conflict Resolution Smarts* and *Safety Smarts* for the USA TODAY Teen Wise Guides series.